The Little Book of My Neighbourhood

by Judith Harrie

Illustrations by Marion Lindsay

LITTLE BOOKS WITH **BIG** IDEAS

Featherstone Education
An imprint of Bloomsbury Publishing Plc

50 Bedford Square
London
WC1B 3DP
UK

1385 Broadway
New York
NY 10018
USA

www.bloomsbury.com

Bloomsbury is a registered trademark of Bloomsbury Publishing Plc

First published 2016

Text ©Judith Harries, 2016
Illustrations ©Marion Lindsay, 2016
Cover photographs ©Shutterstock, 2016

British Library Cataloguing-in-Publication Data
A catalogue record for this book is available from the British Library.

ISBN:
PB 978-1-4729-2507-7
ePDF 978-1-4729-2508-4

Library of Congress Cataloging-in-Publication Data
A catalog record for this book is available from the Library of Congress.

1 3 5 7 9 10 8 6 4 2

Printed and bound in India by Replika Press Pvt. Ltd

This book is produced using paper that is made from wood grown in managed, sustainable forests. It is natural, renewable and recyclable. The logging and manufacturing processes conform to the environmental regulations of the country of origin.

**To view more of our titles please visit
www.bloomsbury.com**

Contents

Introduction

This Little Book seeks to provide early years practitioners with a rich variety of ideas for helping children to explore and understand their local neighbourhood.

The Early Learning Goal for 'Understanding the world' states that 'Children should talk about the features of their own immediate environment', and this starts with the spaces, places and people around them, at home, at nursery school, and in local shops, streets and towns.

Thanks to modern technology, it is now much easier to study the environment, both on our doorstep and further afield. Online maps can show children many different views of their home surroundings and help them to feel more aware of the world around them, and there are many websites that children can visit to view different buildings, animals and people from around the world.

The activities included in this book, mainly focusing on maps, walks, talks, visits and trips, all provide practitioners with lots of opportunities to extend children's learning across many diverse early years topics.

Links with the EYFS framework

The prime areas of learning and development

Communication and language (CL)

Listening and attention

Children will listen to books being read, stories being told and visitors speaking to them, and are encouraged to concentrate and talk about what they hear, responding with relevant comments, questions and actions.

Understanding

Children will follow layered instructions when involved in visits, walks and trips. They answer 'how' and 'why' questions about what they have observed.

Speaking

Children can speak to the group about things that they have seen, heard or felt during activities. They are aware of using past, present and future forms when describing events.

Physical development (PD)

Moving and handling

Many of the activities involve walking to and from places, so children will be encouraged to move confidently and be aware of space. They will be encouraged to handle tools and equipment when making junk models and to use a pencil for writing.

Self-confidence and self-awareness

Children will become more aware of the importance of regular exercise in keeping healthy. An important part of many of the walks and trips will be to increase children's awareness of keeping safe by staying with an assigned adult.

Managing feelings and behaviour

Children have many opportunities to work in small groups. They can show acceptable behaviour when 'out and about' and away from the setting, and are increasingly able to adapt to the changes in routine presented by trips and visits.

The specific areas of learning and development

Literacy (L)

Reading

Children are encouraged to read lots of signs, symbols and posters in their setting and wider environment.

Writing

Children use their phonic knowledge to write their names, high frequency words, and simple sentences.

Mathematics (M)

Numbers

They use counting skills as they observe their environment. They can use tally charts to record results of surveys and compare amounts.

Shape, space and measures

Children use everyday language to talk about size, position, distance, time and money in problem solving. They observe shapes and patterns in their environment and use mathematical language.

Understanding the world (UW)

People and communities

Children are encouraged to talk about their neighbourhood by describing their families, homes and living environment. They compare similarities and differences between their lives and others, and among families, communities and traditions.

The world

All the activities in this Little Book focus on part of this Early Learning Goal, looking at a child's neighbourhood from lots of different angles and perspectives. Children will compare similarities and differences between places, objects, materials and living things. They are encouraged to talk about features of their own immediate environment.

Technology

Lots of activities include suggestions for exciting websites to visit and use, which can be explored via a range of technology.

Exploring and using media and materials

Many activities involve songs and musical ideas. There are lots of creative and design activities exploring a variety of materials, tools and techniques, experimenting with colour, design, texture, form and function.

Being imaginative

Children use media and materials in original ways. They are encouraged to use their own ideas, thoughts and feelings when involved with creative activities especially designing junk models, art, and role play.

How to use this book

This book is divided into four main sections that take the practitioner and the children through a journey around the neighbourhood. It starts with the child's immediate local environment in 'My space', which could be worked through as an introductory unit of work with a new group of children. It explores children's homes and families, before looking at the local street and town environment. The second section suggests a number of organised 'Walks' you can do with your group, and is followed by the section 'Making it real', which is full of ideas for useful visitors to invite to your setting. The final section, 'Special places', offers ideas for specialised trips outside of your setting.

The book can also be used as a complete resource for practitioners to pick and choose activities from, for use alongside topic-based learning. Those planning a topic on animals, for example, would find the activities 'A visit from the vet', 'Minibeast walk' and 'A local farm' very useful!

The activities will help children to discover their own neighbourhood and community in all its rich complexity. The section on visits, 'Making it real', seeks to develop children's understanding of our multi-cultural society by inviting local people to talk about their own customs and heritage. It is important to make the most of the varied heritage of the children in your specific group: for instance, if you have a number of Australian children in your setting, you may wish to devise a 'Visit from Oz' activity, using the ideas in this book as a template.

Each activity includes a list of resources, many of which are common to a wide range of activities – for example, digital cameras, clipboards and drawing materials. This is followed by step-by-step instructions for a range of activities around the topic. Many of the activities require you to obtain parental permission, such as before embarking on a walk or visit. Involving parents as extra adult help for the activities will increase the children's opportunities to learn during the experience. It is also essential to fill out a risk assessment for any trip that takes place away from your setting. Practitioners should always make pre-trip visits to ensure they are aware of any potential health and safety issues.

The 'Further afield' section provides ideas for extending the learning beyond the children's normal experience of their local neighbourhood, by looking at the wider world and making comparisons.

The 'Whatever next?' section provides practitioners with further ideas for how to develop the activity, and usually includes a follow-on activity directly related to the topic. Finally, lots of the activities are concluded with helpful 'Links with the EYFS', to show how they cover various different Early Learning Goals (ELGs). Of course, all the activities are focused on the 'Understanding the world' ELG, but many others are also frequently explored. As children prepare for a walk or trip they should always be encouraged to talk about what they expect to see, hear, or feel, developing their self-confidence as they talk to the group (PSED). They should be regularly encouraged to think of suitable questions to ask visitors (CL). An awareness of how to keep safe away from the setting should be fostered before all the walks and trips (PSED).

Section one: My space

My home

Talk about where children live, and share pictures and create junk models of their homes.

What you need:

▶ Photos of children's houses/flats (they can bring these in from home)

▶ Paper, pencils

▶ Easel, paints, brushes

▶ Junk materials – different-sized boxes, tubes, cardboard etc.

What you do:

► Ask children to bring in a photograph of their house or flat. Remind them to write their name on the back.

► Talk about the different types of houses, flats and apartments that they live in. Be sensitive to children who may live between two homes.

► Encourage children to talk about what they like about their home. How many rooms are there? Have they got a garden? Do they share a bedroom with a sibling?

► Sing the traditional song 'Wind the bobbin up' and talk about different parts of a room – ceiling, floor, window, door, etc.

► Let children choose their own materials for making a picture of their home – sketching with pencils or painting at the easel.

► Use the photograph and their observations to create a model of their home with a variety of junk materials. Empty, clean, cardboard milk cartons can be transformed into model houses with ready-made roofs. Assist children with cutting out windows and doors.

► Can they write the number or name of the house or flat onto their artwork?

► Play the game 'Here's my House'. Call out different types of homes and ask children to carry out different actions for each, for example:

▷ 'terraced' – stand in a row and link arms

▷ 'bungalow' – drop to the floor

▷ 'flat' – reach up on tiptoes

▷ 'semi-detached' – find a partner and link arms

▷ 'detached' – stand in a place and make a roof with arms

▷ 'caravan' – move arms like wheels

▷ 'tent' – drop to floor and make a tent shape.

Further afield:

► Look at different types of buildings that people in the UK live in, such as cottages, terraced houses, blocks of flats, high rise apartments, above shops, house boats, mobile homes, stately homes, castles, and so on.

► Compare these with buildings that people in different countries live in, such as igloos, teepees, tree houses, yurts, log cabins, houses on stilts, mud houses, caves or even underground. Read *Home* by Kate Petty (in the Oxfam Around the World series). Try making models of different types of houses.

Whatever next?

Read *My New Home* by Marta Altes, which is all about moving house. Moving can be an unsettling time for young children. Role play moving house with them: pack up everything in the home corner into boxes, then move it to another part of the setting and unpack everything again, but set it all out differently, to help the children get used to the concept of change.

Links with the EYFS

Related themes – Houses and homes; Ourselves

PSED: Encourage children to be sensitive to others as they share details about their homes. Try to discourage negative comparisons.

CL: Enjoy sharing books about different types of homes.

M: Try counting the number of rooms in their home. Compare with the number of people. Do they know the number of their house?

EAD: Sing along with 'Our House' by Madness.

My bedroom

Talk about children's bedrooms, make floor plans and challenge them to design a new and improved bedroom!

What you need:

- Copy of *The Bedroom* by Van Gogh
- Dolls' house furniture
- Shoeboxes
- Paint colour charts
- Wallpaper books
- Catalogues

What you do:

- Talk to children about their bedroom at home. Can they describe the furniture or decoration in their room? What do they have on the walls? Do they share their bedroom with a sibling?

▶ Look at Van Gogh's painting 'The Bedroom'. Ask children to paint a picture of their bedroom from memory.

▶ Ask them to make a floor plan of their room. Demonstrate by drawing a floor plan of the classroom, as a guide. Can they use the miniature dolls' house furniture to create a model layout of their own room?

▶ Explain that they are going to design a new bedroom in a shoebox. Help children to cut windows and a door out of the sides of the box. Leave the left side of each window or door uncut so they can be opened and closed.

▶ Decorate the floor with a fabric rug and the walls with wallpaper or wrapping paper. Cut out pictures of furniture and toys to add to the room, or construct furniture out of paper or cardboard boxes. Cut out tiny paintings or posters to decorate the walls.

Further afield:

▶ Look at different types of beds such as hammocks, canopy beds and bunk beds. Can children tell you about their bed at home? Bring in a hammock for children to take turns using during story time.

Whatever next?

Play the game 'Move me', using a soft toy: ask for a volunteer to give directions to another child to move a soft toy around the room. Can they move the toy from the teacher's desk to the door, or from the top of the bookcase to the sink, for example? The rules are that they are only allowed to move when given directions, for instance: "Take three steps forwards; turn left at the home corner; take one step back; bend down", etc.

Links with the EYFS

Related themes – Houses and homes; Ourselves

M: Look at repeated patterns in wallpaper designs.

CL: Read *The Magic Bed* by John Burningham. Talk about different types of beds. Do any of the children think they have a magic bed? Where would they dream about going?

EAD: Children can develop their artistic skills by looking at famous artists' work, painting their own pictures and designing new bedrooms.

My address

Help children to remember their home addresses and to find them on a local map.

What you need:

▶ A list of children's addresses written on postcards

▶ Access to Google Maps

▶ Photos of children's homes (see 'My home', page 8)

▶ Salt and flour dough

What you do:

▶ Ask children if they know their address already. Can they remember the house number or the name of the road?

▶ Think of ways to help children remember their own address – links with other words, rhymes, places, etc.

- ▶ Provide each child with their address written down on a postcard. Help them to read their own and each other's addresses.
- ▶ On an interactive white board or computer, go to Google Maps and look at the local area. If this is not possible display an enlarged copy of a local paper map.
- ▶ Show the children where the setting is on the map.
- ▶ Invite the children to show you where their address is on the map. Change to the street view. Can they see their house?
- ▶ Identify other local features such as churches, shops, library, parks, etc.
- ▶ Switch between the map, the street view and the satellite view. Which view do the children like best?
- ▶ Print, enlarge and display a copy of the local map on the wall. Invite children to stick the photo of their house in the correct location.

Further afield:

- ▶ Look at maps of other local towns or familiar places on Google Maps. Compare with the local area.
- ▶ Talk about other significant addresses that the children may know or wish to know – grandparents, friends and other members of their families. Do they know any famous addresses e.g. Number 10 Downing Street.

Whatever next?
Give the children some salt and flour dough to create a door plaque for their house. Roll out the dough to a thickness of 1cm and cut into an oval or rectangle shape. Press magnetic letters into the dough to write the house name or stick on numbers that the children have crafted from the dough. Bake at 100°C until dried out, then leave to cool, paint and varnish.

Links with the EYFS

Related themes – Ourselves; Houses and homes

PSED: Emphasise to children the importance of knowing their own address, but that they should only share this information with grown ups they trust, i.e. not strangers.

CL: Children can talk about where they live in relation to others, friends, family and setting.

L: Children can write their own address on an envelope or postcard.

M: Look at how many children in the group live on a particular street. Is one road very popular? Talk about the distance between home and nursery school (see 'My journey to nursery school', page 23).

My garden

Use collage materials to create a fantasy garden with the children, and open a garden centre in the role-play area!

What you need:

- Photos of children's gardens
- Paper and pencils
- Catalogues
- Scissors

What you do:

- Talk about children's gardens at home. Can they describe their garden? Let them share pictures of their gardens and say what they like to do in the garden. Be aware that some children may not have access to a garden, so they could talk about a local park or recreation area.

- Make a list of things children would like to have in their garden: grass, football goal, flowers, sand pit, trampoline, swing, hammock, trees to climb, etc.
- Create a fantasy 'My garden' picture with the children using photo, drawings and collage materials. Frame these and display them.
- Grow some flowers from seeds with the children that they can start off at in the setting and then take home in small pots to care for at home or in their garden. Good ones to try are sunflowers, marigolds, nasturtiums or morning glory.
- Set up a garden centre in the role-play area. Provide wellington boots, gardening tools, spades, gloves, magazines, packets of seeds, different-sized plant pots, watering cans, garden furniture, toys, buckets, lawn mower and wheelbarrows.
- Make small pot plants to sell by stuffing a flower pot with shredded brown tissue paper and adding a plant or flower cut out of card/material on top.

Further afield:

- Look at pictures online of gardens in the UK such as Kew Gardens, Hidcote Manor Garden, the topiary garden in Beckley or the Lost Gardens of Heligan.
- Look at styles of gardens in other countries – Japanese botanical gardens, Claude Monet's garden in France, or Mughal gardens in India.

Whatever next?

Dig a small flowerbed in your outside area. Let children plan which flowers they are going to plant. Try bedding plants in spring or grow your own from seeds. Organise a rota for children to water the flowers.

Links with the EYFS

Related themes – Houses and homes; Ourselves; Plants; Growth

CL: Children can develop speaking and listening skills in the role-play garden centre. Enjoy sharing books about gardening, such as *Eddie's Garden* by Sarah Garland, and *Jasper's Beanstalk* by Mick Inkpen.

PD: Children can develop handling skills by using tools in the garden.

EAD: Sing the traditional song 'Mary, Mary quite contrary'. Change the words to include the children's names and different flowers.

My maps

Look at maps of the local area online, and create laminated map placemats.

What you need:

- ▶ A list of children's addresses
- ▶ Access to Google Maps
- ▶ Local maps or a copy of an *A to Z*
- ▶ Laminator

What you do:

- ▶ Look at maps of the local area on IWB via Google Maps or Streetmap. Show children different views – map, street view, aerial view, etc.
- ▶ Look at photos of the area linked to the map. Show children how to zoom in and out and different ways to use the maps online.
- ▶ Give children a paper map or a copy of an *A to Z* of the local area.

- Take screen captures of an online map or photocopy an enlarged paper map that shows each child's address.
- Print onto A4 sized sheets of paper. Ask each child to make a small drawing of their house and stick onto the correct position on the map. Laminate the maps to create a placemat that the children can take home.
- Play some games to familiarise children with left and right – ask them to place their hands palm down on the table: left hand will make the shape of a 'L' for left.
- Shoes are a good place to start when teaching children left and right. If children know how to read their names then you can write half of their name in the left shoe and the second half inside the right shoe. Drawing half of a smiley face in each shoe is another good way to teach this.
- Sing the 'Hokey Cokey' and practise using left and right arms and legs. Ask children to listen to the GPS or SatNav in their cars when it gives directions to turn left and right.

Further afield:

- Provide the children with an atlas, a globe and maps from around the world. Display a world map and ask the children to find the UK. Look at the relative size of countries and oceans. Go to www.barefootworldatlas.com and let them explore the magical interactive 3D globe.

Whatever next?

Try playing 'Blindfold Pairs'. Ask children to find a partner and then blindfold one of them. Explain that they are going to provide directions for their partner, rather like a Satnav. Can the sighted partner give their blindfolded friend instructions to move safely around the room avoiding furniture and any other obstacles? Encourage them to use left and right directions.

Links with the EYFS

Related themes – Houses and homes; Ourselves

PSED: Emphasise to children the importance of knowing their own address, but that they should only share this information with grown ups they trust, i.e. not strangers.

CL: Children should talk about where they live in relation to others, friends, family and setting.

PD: Children can practise their co-ordination and physical skills.

My family

Talk about families and create a family tree. Invite a mother with a new baby to visit the setting.

What you need:

▶ Information about children's families

▶ Family tree template – a big, leafy tree with white stickers to add for family members

▶ Baby photos of children and staff

What you do:

▶ Talk to children about their families. How many people are in their immediate family? Be sure to include all types of families – single parents, heterosexual couples, homosexual couples, parents who live separately, adopted children, etc.

- Show the children an example of a family tree. Use your own family as an example, showing siblings, mums and dads, grandmas and grandads.
- Encourage children to bring in photos of their families at family celebrations or holidays. Ask them to paint portraits of their families. Mount and display these around your setting.
- Provide children with a template of a family tree with lots of blank circular stickers for them to add to the branches. Ask them to draw pictures and help them to write the names of members of their family onto the stickers.
- Invite a mother with a new baby to come into your setting and talk to the children about having a new baby in the family. Let the children think of questions to ask about the baby and how to care for him or her.
- In small groups let the children watch the baby having a bath or nappy change.
- Ask children to design and make some new baby cards for children whose families are expecting a new arrival.

Further afield:

- Many children in early years experience the arrival of a new baby into their family. Read *There's a House Inside my Mummy* by Giles Andreae or *We're Having a Super Baby* by Abie Longstaff, and share some of the different feelings this can create.

Whatever next?

Make a display of baby photos of the children and staff. See how many photos the children can identify. How have they changed since they were babies? Try this as a competition inviting parents and carers to get involved and raise some funds.

Links with the EYFS

Related themes – Ourselves; Families; Growth

PSED: Read *Who's in my Family?* by Robie H. Harris, which offers a good introduction to the different families that make up our society.

CL: Enjoy sharing books about families and new babies, such as *What's in your tummy, Mummy?* by Sam Lloyd and *There's a House inside my Mummy* by Giles Andreae.

EAD: Design and make new baby cards using a variety of materials.

My neighbours

Introduce the idea of charity and helping others, starting with our neighbours.

What you need:

► Friendly neighbours!

► A local or national charity representative

► Card, pens, collage materials

What you do:

► Talk to the children about the word 'neighbours'. Who are their neighbours? How can they be friendly to their neighbours? Contrast neighbours with strangers; remind children about 'stranger danger' and that they shouldn't talk to people that they don't know.

- ▶ Talk about the work of different charities who help people with a variety of needs. If appropriate, relate this to the children in your setting. For instance, if you have a child who is visually impaired invite a representative from the RNIB to come and talk to the children.
- ▶ Arrange a visit from a local charity worker who is happy to come and talk to the children about the work that they do.
- ▶ Write thank you letters and make thank you cards to send to the charity visitor.
- ▶ Organise some fund raising events for the charity that the children are learning about. Try hosting a sponsored silence, circuits, cake stall, MUFTI day, etc.
- ▶ Read or tell the story of 'The Good Samaritan' from the Bible. Act out the story. Sing 'When I needed a neighbour were you there?'. Invite parents to come and watch this as an assembly on 'Neighbours'.
- ▶ Talk about different ways children could 'help their neighbours' – looking after pets, sharing things, making cakes, playing with children, etc.

Further afield:

- ▶ Go to www.charitychoice.co.uk and find out about charities in your local area.
- ▶ Get involved in national charity campaigns such as Comic Relief, Sport Relief and Children in Need.

Whatever next?

Make 'Love your neighbour' badges for the children to wear. Arrange to visit the people who live next door to the setting – the neighbours. Bake some biscuits or fairy cakes and take them round to the properties next to the setting. Invite them to setting events.

Links with the EYFS

Related themes – Ourselves; Houses and homes

PSED: Children can show sensitivity to others needs and feelings and form positive relationships with adults and other children.

CL: Children can listen attentively to your visitor and ask appropriate questions.

My journey to nursery school

Talk about how the children travel to your setting, and discuss their journeys. Locate the setting and their home addresses on a giant map.

What you need:

- ▶ Access to Google Maps
- ▶ Enlarged copies of local maps
- ▶ Coloured pencils

What you do:

- ▶ Talk about where the children live and look at some addresses on Google Maps or an enlarged copy of a local map. Can the children remember their addresses? (See 'My address', page 13.)

▶ Point out where the setting is on the map. Look at the relative distances that different children travel to get to nursery school. Who travels the furthest? Who lives the closest?

▶ Choose an address that is not too far from your setting and talk about the route they would take to reach setting. On an enlarged paper map, show the children how to draw a line showing their route in red.

▶ Talk about the different ways children can travel to nursery school – walk, bus, car, bike, etc. What do they pass on their way?

▶ Provide each child with an enlarged copy of a local map. Help them to draw their route to setting on the map.

▶ Conduct a survey to see what is the most popular way to come to the setting.

▶ Visit pbskids.org/arthur/games/gogeorgego online and try programming Arthur's journeys.

Further afield:

▶ Talk about other journeys that the children have made. How many different countries have the children visited? Display a world map and pin flags on the countries that they have been to. Don't forget to include your own travels.

> ## Whatever next?
> Join in with the Living Streets UK 'Walk to School' week in May each year, and encourage more children to walk to your setting. Emphasise the benefits of walking as a regular exercise.

Links with the EYFS
Related themes – Setting; Ourselves; Journeys
PSED: Emphasise to children the importance of knowing their own address, but that they should only share this information with grown ups they trust, i.e. not strangers.

CL: Share a book about a different kind of journey, i.e. *Lost and Found* by Oliver Jeffers.

M: Children can use tally marks to count and calculate how children travel to the setting.

PD: Children should appreciate the importance of physical exercise for good health.

My nursery school

Make large labelled plans of the setting and then create giant models using junk materials.

What you need:

- Simple architectural plans of your nursery or setting
- Large pieces of paper, pencils, pens, and rulers
- Junk materials – different-sized boxes, tubes, cardboard, etc.
- Scissors, glue, tape

What you do:

- Go on a walk around your setting, inside and outside. Is it big or small? Is the roof sloped or flat? Is there a playground, garden, outside area, football pitch, field, flower bed, trees, etc.

- ▶ How many different rooms are there inside? Is there a kitchen, office, gym, hall, library, music room, etc.
- ▶ Show the children the plans of the setting. If the architectural plans are complicated, produce your own simplified version to share with them.
- ▶ Ask children to draw their own plans of the setting on large pieces of paper using pencils, pens and rulers. Can they label the different rooms? Which room will be the biggest?
- ▶ Can they draw a more detailed plan or layout of the setting marking windows, furniture, role-play area, home corner, book corner, writing table, water tray, etc? What else would they like to include to improve the environment?
- ▶ Put the children in small groups to create giant models of the setting. Provide them with different-sized boxes, glue and tape. Offer help with cutting windows, doors and joining tricky parts together. Paint the models and display finished artwork.
- ▶ Talk about nursery rules and how they are important in keeping everyone safe and happy. What happens if people break the rules?

Further afield:

- ▶ Look at images of different types of nursery school buildings in photos or online.
- ▶ Organise a link with a nursery school overseas, either through the British Council 'Connecting Classrooms' partnership, or through Oxfam's 'School Partnerships' scheme.

Whatever next?

With the children, make a list of all the people who work in your setting and the different jobs that they do. Let them think of some questions to ask the staff. Arrange for them to interview the teachers, head, secretary, site supervisor, dinner lady, etc.

Links with the EYFS

Related themes – Jobs people do; Setting; Ourselves

PSED: Children can work as part of a group to understand and follow the rules.

CL: Share some books together about settings such as *Starting School* by Allan Ahlberg or *I am too Absolutely Small for School* by Lauren Child.

My street

Look at photos of streets in your neighbourhood, then go on a local walk. Ask the children to create a collage of a street, complete with their choice of buildings and features.

What you need:

- Photos of local streets
- Property and car newspapers
- Black sugar paper, chalk, cardboard

What you do:

- Show the children the photos of the local streets. Talk about things that they recognise – houses, trees, shops, buildings, cars, and so on.
- What do the children like about their street? Is it quiet so they can play out? Are there trees and flowers in the front gardens? Is there a shop that sells sweets or a fish and chips café? Do they like the name of their street?

- ▶ What don't they like about their street? It is noisy or dirty? Is the traffic busy? Is it a long way from nursery school or grandma's/grandad's house?
- ▶ Go on a short walk down the street where your setting is situated. Take photos of buildings, signs, objects, etc.
- ▶ Look for things to count such as cars, keyholes, manhole covers, lamp posts, chimneys, red doors, fences, postboxes, garages, etc.
- ▶ Give each child a thin strip of black paper. Ask them to cut out pictures of houses and other buildings, cars, trees and stick them along the paper to create a street. They can choose which buildings and services they would like to include in their street. Add lines on the road with chalks – broken white lines, double yellow lines, parking bays, etc. Can they think of a name for their street and create a label or sign for it?
- ▶ Set out a street play mat and lots of toy vehicles. Talk about routes cars can take to different places or buildings. Which are the fastest routes?

Further afield:

- ▶ Look at images of paintings by L.S. Lowry of his neighbourhood – 'A Village Square' or 'Coming out of Setting', the works of Ton Schulten – 'Lighted City' and Banksy – street art. Let children have a go at painting on the wall outside using chalks and water. (Don't worry, it will all wash away!)

Whatever next?

Let children complete a traffic survey of the cars, lorries, buses, bikes that pass by the setting. Which is the most popular colour of car? What is the most unusual vehicle they spot? Make a pictogram showing the results. Challenge children to spot and write down number plates on cars as they pass. Who can find a number plate with a 1, 2, 3 etc on it?

Links with the EYFS

Related themes – Jobs people do; Setting; Ourselves

CL: Read *The High Street* by Alice Melvin. Talk about the different buildings in the book. How many of them are similar to buildings in your street?

M: Using a tally chart to work out numbers for the traffic survey will develop children's counting skills.

My town

Look at photos of your local town, then walk around town together.
Back in the setting, work in groups to create a model town or village.
Open 'shops' in your role-play area!

What you need:

▶ Photos of your village, town or city

▶ Junk materials – different-sized boxes, tubes, cardboard, etc.

▶ Scissors, glue, tape

What you do:

▶ Look at photos of your village, town or city. Do the children recognise any of the pictures? Can they name any of the buildings?

▶ Go for a walk around the town. Talk about significant features of the area - village green, park or green space, pub, cafe, setting, church, shops, museum, town hall, car park, market, factory, etc.

- ▶ Discuss features of buildings. Do they have large windows to show goods? Are there signs to tell people what they are? Take photos of a variety of buildings.
- ▶ Ask children to work together in pairs to make models of different buildings to create a model village or town. Create an interactive display with small world figures that the children can play with.
- ▶ Make a list of different types of shops and services in the town – supermarket, grocer, greengrocer, butcher, baker, chemist, shoe, clothes, hat, newsagent, cheese, deli, toy, jewellery, book, hairdresser, café, post office, library, etc. Can the children tell you what all the types of shops sell?
- ▶ Choose a couple of contrasting shops to open in the role-play area. You could create a shoe shop with lots of different types of shoes, boxes, measuring equipment, bags, mirror, shoe cleaning equipment, comfy chairs and cushions, cash register, money, cards, etc.
- ▶ Open a cafe with kitchen equipment, tables, chairs, printed menus, notepad and pen, various food, and dressing up uniforms, aprons, chef's hats, etc. Encourage children to engage in role play in the café as a waitress, cook, or customer.

Further afield:

- ▶ Go to www.bbc.co.uk/settingradio/subjects/earlylearning and listen to sounds from outside for children to identify – a police siren, footsteps, children playing, clock chimes, traffic, etc.

Whatever next?
Talk about the local town newspaper and the different sections – news stories, adverts, property, cars, etc. Ask the children to help think of news they would like to tell the group. Scribe some of their ideas and create a setting newspaper for the week.

Links with the EYFS
Related themes – Jobs people do; Setting; Ourselves
PSED: Children are confident to speak in a familiar group.

CL: Share some stories about shops such as *The World-Famous Cheese Shop Break-in* by Sean Taylor, or *Happy Street: Cafe/Supermarket/Bookshop/Toyshop* by Simon Abbott.

PD: Children know how to keep safe when away from the setting.

Take-away Bear

Introduce the Take-away Bear to the children and invite them to take turns spending time with the bear at home or on outings.

What you need:

▶ A suitable teddy bear or soft toy

▶ Back pack with teddy's clothes, diary, and toothbrush

What you do:

▶ Introduce the Take-away Bear to the children and explain that they are going to take turns to take him or her home with them for a weekend or overnight stay.

▶ Explain that they can record in Bear's diary what they get up to including drawings, photos and writing.

- Take care to reassure the parents that they don't need to arrange 'special' outings, just let Bear join in with normal evening or weekend activities. Some parents can get quite competitive!
- However, if a child is going somewhere special for a holiday it might be worth asking if Bear can accompany them so they can share the experience with their friends when they return!
- When each child returns with Take-away Bear let them share with the group what they got up to, reading out his diary and showing any pictures.
- Keep a class record of the Bear's activities in a scrapbook for children and parents to look at and talk about.
- Make sure every child has a turn with Take-away Bear during the term or year.

Further afield:

- Go to www.travelingteddybear.com and find out about the Traveling Teddy Bears project – another well-travelled bear who links settings and classrooms across the world.
- Check out Jofli bears (Journey of Life) that are used to help children record memories, are often helpful to those who are going through emotional turmoil.

Whatever next?

Involve Take-away Bear in other group activities such as walks and visits. Try producing a film of Bear away on his own somewhere for children to watch. This could be used to introduce new topics or teaching points. For instance, to promote healthy eating Bear could be filmed at the shops with a basket of healthy food or sitting on the beach eating a healthy picnic.

Links with the EYFS

Related themes – Bears; Toys; Holidays; Food

PSED: Children share their experience with Take-away Bear, become more aware of others' needs and feelings, and can speak confidently to the group.

CL: Share some books about Bears such as *Where's my Teddy?* by Jez Alborough and *Bears Don't Read* by Emma Chichester Clark.

Section two: Walks

A spy walk

Go on a walk around the local neighbourhood looking for different things to spy on such as numbers, letters, shapes, buildings – and each other!

What you need:

▶ Clipboards, paper and pens

▶ Digital camera

▶ Magnifying glasses

What you do:

▶ Plan a walk around your neighbourhood where the children will be able to spot lots of different things. Decide and plan what aspect of the neighbourhood you want them to 'spy' on before leaving the setting. You may choose to focus on numbers, letters, shapes – or something more unusual!

▶ Show the children the route you are planning to take on a local map.

▶ Talk to the children about what they should observe during the walk. Provide them with lists of specific things to look for like a treasure hunt.

▶ Try a numbers walk. Look for house numbers, car registration plates, posters in shops, signs on buildings, adverts with prices, traffic speed signs, etc.

▶ Try a shapes walk. Look for windows, buildings, traffic signs – (triangles and circles), posters and signs on shops, etc.

▶ Try a letters walk. Can the children spot any letters they recognise such as their initial letters? Look for shop names and signs, street names, car registration plates, signs on vans, advertisements, posters, etc.

▶ As you walk along, ask children to keep looking carefully at what is around them all the time. When they see an item on their list they must stop, identify it and make a note on the clipboard.

▶ Ask them to take note of any unexpected, surprising or funny things that they see. Use the digital camera to record these.

Further afield:

▶ Talk about the seven wonders of the world and show the children images of them online.

▶ Go to www.passmytheory.co.uk and look at all the different road signs. What is the difference between the triangle signs (warnings) and the circle signs (orders).

Whatever next?

Look at images of street, shop and road signs. Talk about the different shapes and fonts used in the signs. Let the children design signs for different parts of your setting – the writing table, role-play areas, reading corner, etc. Let them use ICT to product signs using large font sizes and bright colours or design their own, scribe and enlarge on the photocopier. Print and laminate the best signs.

Links with the EYFS

Related themes – People who help us; Buildings; Numbers; Shapes

PSED: Talk about the importance of keeping together as a group when away from your setting.

L: Children can link sounds to letters, naming and sounding letters of the alphabet.

M: Children can use mathematical language to describe any shapes that they spy.

A sound walk

Go on a walk around the local neighbourhood listening out for different things such as traffic, people and animals.

What you need:

▶ Phone or tablet to record sounds
▶ Clipboards, paper and pens
▶ Musical instruments

What you do:

▶ Plan a walk around your neighbourhood where the children will be able to hear lots of different sounds from traffic, people, animals, building, etc.

- ▶ Show the children the route you are planning to take on a local map.
- ▶ Talk to the children about what they expect to hear during the walk.
- ▶ As you walk along, ask children to keep listening carefully all the time. When they hear a sound they must stop, identify it and make a note on the clipboard.
- ▶ Are there any mysterious sounds that cannot be identified? Try to record some sounds so you can listen to them again back at your setting.
- ▶ Back at the setting make a list of all the different sounds the children identified. Which sound was the most frequently heard?
- ▶ Ask children to sit very quietly and listen to sounds around them in your setting. Can the children identify them all? Are there any surprise sounds?
- ▶ Play some listening games using recorded sounds or instrument sounds. Can the children play back a string of two or three contrasting sounds on instruments? Try tambourine, wood block and triangle.

Further afield:

- ▶ Go to www.bbc.co.uk/settingradio/earlylearning and search for Stimulus Sounds Library. This site has lots of sound effects to listen to and use with the children.

> ### Whatever next?
> Read or tell the children a story with lots of scope for sound effects such as 'The Three Little Pigs' - building, blowing, falling down sounds. Help children to use voices, body percussion or musical instruments to create sound effects to play along with the story. Film the children acting out the story with sound effects.

Links with the EYFS

Related themes – Animals; Sounds

PSED: Talk about the importance of keeping together as a group when away from your setting.

CL: Read some *Sounds of the Wild* books by Maurice Pledger, together with sound effects!

EAD: Children can experiment with ways of making and changing sounds.

A walk to the park in spring

Go on a lively group walk to the park and experience the outdoor space using all available senses.

What you need:

▶ Permission from parents/carers to go on a walk

▶ Extra adults to accompany your group, to increase the effectiveness of learning opportunities

▶ Sketch pads, or clipboards and paper

▶ Digital camera

▶ Empty bags to collect found items

What you do:

▶ Before you leave the setting, talk to the group about what you expect to see, hear, smell and do on the walk.

▶ Give the children a list of spring things to spot such as new buds on plants, blossom flowers, nests, minibeasts, birds, and so on. Encourage the children to make sketches of the things they see.

▶ Ask the children to stop and listen to sounds around them in the park. Can they make a list of sounds or record them on a phone to talk about later? Can they hear any birds singing? Back in your setting, listen to examples of birdsong online on Birdsong FM.

▶ See if you can spot a bird's nest in a tree to show the children. Collect materials in the park to build your own nests. Look out for twigs, dry grass, lichen, moss, etc.

▶ If the weather is fine, find a sheltered place and ask children to attempt to build nest structures out of the items they found. Can they make their nest with one hand, like a bird using its beak? Take photos of the children's nests.

▶ Place nests in the branches of trees and leave them for birds to adopt! Alternatively, if the weather is bad, let children carry their treasures in bags back to the setting before making the nests.

Further afield:

▶ Talk about the sounds the children heard in the park – birds singing, bees buzzing, squirrels rustling, cuckoos calling, children laughing, raindrops falling, etc. Use voices and instruments to copy the sounds and create a 'Spring Symphony'.

Whatever next?
Go online and look at the work of British artist Andy Goldsworthy, who creates sculptures using found objects. Encourage the children to organise their found items into patterns, shapes and pictures. Photograph their creations.

Links with the EYFS
Related themes – Seasons; Weather; Birds
PSED: Talk about the importance of keeping together as a group when away from your setting.

PD: Talk about the importance of exercise for keeping healthy.

CL: Encourage the use of new words to describe what the children see on the walk.

M: Children can practise number skills, e.g. finding two birds or three flowers.

EAD: Children can show evidence of using mixed media and imagination.

A summer picnic

Enjoy a picnic at the park, then create a model playground containing all the children's favourite rides.

What you need:

▶ A local park with a safe playground
▶ Picnic food, rugs
▶ Appropriate clothes for hot weather
▶ Junk modelling equipment

What you do:

▶ Choose a suitable park, field or garden to walk to for your picnic. Show the children where the picnic spot is on a local map.
▶ Make sure children are aware of how to dress and keep safe in the sun – sun hats, suncream, lots of drinks, etc.

▶ Talk about the picnic with the children and make a list of ideas for food and drinks.

▶ Involve the children in making sandwiches for the picnic, spreading butter on bread, choosing fillings and cutting the sandwiches into small squares and triangles.

▶ At the park, let children choose different rides to try out. Talk about the names of the equipment – roundabouts, slides, swings, see-saw, monkey bars, trim trail, etc.

▶ What is the children's favourite ride at the park? Create a pictogram to show the results of your survey.

▶ Enjoy sharing food and drink at the picnic. Sing the 'Teddy Bear's Picnic' song.

▶ Try some group games in the park if the weather allows such as 'Duck Duck Goose' or 'Stuck in the Mud'.

▶ Create a plan for a model of your playground with all the different equipment. Back in your setting, let the children work together to make moving models of some of the play equipment using junk, string, split pins, etc.

Further afield:

▶ Look at L.S. Lowry's famous painting, 'The Playground'. Make a list of the different rides the children can see in the picture. Compare these with the playground they have visited. Can they paint a picture of the park they visited?

Whatever next?

Talk with the children about how the different play equipment works. Look at pictures of the children using the equipment. How do the different pieces move, with a push or a pull? How does it stop? Can the roundabout go faster? Ask children to design their own fantasy playground with all their favourite rides and new ones that they have thought of themselves.

Links with the EYFS

Related themes – Seasons; Weather; Minibeasts; Food

PSED: Talk about the importance of keeping together as a group when away from your setting.

M: Ask children to use mathematical language to describe shapes of sandwiches and play equipment.

EAD: Sing the 'Teddy Bear's Picnic' song.

A walk to the park in autumn

Take a trip to the park and collect some natural treasures to create autumnal art.

What you need:

▶ Permission from parents/carers to go on a walk

▶ Extra adults to accompany children to increase effectiveness of learning opportunities

▶ Digital camera

▶ Empty bags for 'Collectors'

▶ Magnifying glasses

▶ Sketch books or clipboards and paper

What you do:

▶ Before you leave the setting talk to the children and adults about what you expect to see, hear, smell and do on the walk.

▶ Explain that you want to collect evidence of the changes in the environment since the last walk – changing colours, fallen leaves, berries, footprints, spiders' webs, etc.

▶ Explain that you want to collect evidence of the changes in the environment since the last walk – changing colours, fallen leaves, berries, footprints, spiders' webs, etc.

▶ Make sure that all the children have a bag to collect interesting autumn items in as they walk. Ask them to especially look out for coloured leaves, acorns, conkers, moss, twigs, feathers, bark, etc. Remind them not to pick up any litter and to ask you if they are unsure whether an item is safe.

▶ Back at your setting, let the children use their collections to create some autumn art – you might like to try sketches, collages stuck to thick card or wood, leaf rubbing or printing.

▶ Try creating some 'Wiggly Walk and Talk Sticks' at the park. Choose a natural stick or twig from the park (or take one from the garden) – one with lots of bumps and bends will work best. Let children select special found items to attach to the stick using coloured wool or string. These can be used as a physical 'map' or reminder of the walk.

▶ Take photos of the walk and encourage children to make observational drawings. Combine these with the sticks into a display back at your setting, with added captions written by the children.

Further afield:

▶ Look at photos of autumn or 'fall' online – parts of the US such as New England are well known for stunning autumnal displays.

Whatever next?

Spiders' webs are often most visible at this time of year, highlighted by misty dew. Look out for some on the walk and take photos. Let children observe them through magnifying glasses. Can they draw the pattern of the spider's webs with chalk on black paper? Make spider's web dream catchers by squeezing PVA glue in a web pattern onto round plastic lids, sprinkling on glitter and then leave to dry. Peel off the webs and hang on the windows.

Links with the EYFS

Related themes – Colours; Weather; Minibeasts

PSED: Talk about the importance of keeping together as a group when away from your setting.

CL: Share some stories about parks, such as *Percy the Park Keeper* by Nick Butterworth and *Squirrel's Busy Day* by Lucy Barnard.

PD: Talk about the importance of exercise for keeping healthy.

EAD: There are lots of opportunities for a variety of creative activities using collections of autumn items.

A wintry walk

Let the children experience the beauty of winter weather, and encourage them to take photos of different winter scenes.

What you need:

▶ Permission from parents/carers to take children for a walk

▶ Extra adults to accompany children to increase effectiveness of learning opportunities

▶ Sketch pads or clipboards and paper

▶ Magnifying glasses

▶ Digital camera

▶ Suitable clothes

What you do:

▶ Before you leave your setting, talk to the group about what you expect to see, hear, smell and do on the walk.

- ▶ Talk about the weather on the day of the walk and the appropriate clothing required. Have the children got warm coats, gloves, hats and scarves?
- ▶ If it's very cold outside try some warming up activities – jumping up and down, rubbing hands together, etc. Can the children see their breath in the air as they breathe out?
- ▶ Look for evidence of ice or frost on the grass or fallen leaves. Look at the patterns close-up using magnifying glasses. Ask the children to draw sketches of what they see.
- ▶ Point out the bare trees in winter. Use the correct language – deciduous trees lose their leaves in autumn. Contrast them with the evergreen trees that keep their needle-like leaves all the year around.
- ▶ If there is snow, let the children spend some time building snowmen or snow sculptures.
- ▶ Take photos of the winter scenes – bare trees, children in the snow, footprints, icicles, frost on leaves or grass, etc.

Further afield:

- ▶ Talk to the children about winter in the southern hemisphere at the other side of the world. Show them pictures of Christmas on the beach in Australia! Bring in a globe and point out where we live in comparison to Australia.

Whatever next?

Talk about animals that hibernate over winter. Read some stories about hibernation. Try It was a *Cold Dark Night* by Tim Hopgood, where Ned the hedgehog is looking for somewhere warm to hibernate – or *Don't Wake Up the Bear* by Marjorie Dennis Murray, in which lots of different animals find shelter in Bear's cosy den.

Links with the EYFS

Related themes – Seasons and Weather

PSED: Talk about the importance of keeping together as a group when away from your setting.

PD: Talk about the importance of exercise for keeping healthy.

CL: Share the wintry story about Percy the Park Keeper in *One Snowy Night* by Nick Butterworth. Act out the story using a duvet in the home corner and all the animals coming to get cosy in Percy's hut.

A walk to the postbox

Support the children in writing letters home, then go on a group walk to post them!

What you need:

▶ Permission from parents/carers to take the children for a walk

▶ Extra adults to accompany children to increase effectiveness of learning opportunities

▶ Access to Google Maps

What you do:

▶ Talk to the children about the postal service. What do postal workers do? Do the children enjoy receiving letters or cards through the post?

- Find out where the nearest postbox to your setting is. Talk to the children about postboxes. Is there one near their house?
- Look at the local area on Google Maps. Print off the map and mark the locations of the local postboxes with a red postbox-shaped sticker (or add pins to the map online). As a group, decide which is the nearest postbox to your school.
- Ask the children to bring in a pre-stamped envelope from home. Help them to write a letter or make a card for someone at home and put it inside the envelope.
- Talk to the children about their addresses (see 'My address' on page 13). Help each child to write his or her name and address clearly on the envelope. Make sure all envelopes are sealed.
- Go on a group walk to the nearest post box so the children can post their letters. If possible, arrange to arrive when the postal worker is due to collect the letters so the children can see how it works.
- Ask the children to let you know when their letters arrive at home. Whose letter arrives first – or do they all arrive on the same day?

Further afield:

- In the writing corner, provide lots of varied writing equipment and encourage the children to write letters and draw pictures to send to each other.
- Visit www.penpalschools.com and set up a penpal for your class or setting.

> ### Whatever next?
> At Christmas, make a postbox for your setting from cardboard boxes, painted red with a slit cut in the top. Invite the children to use it to post their Christmas cards to each other. Remind them to write the name of their friend clearly on each envelope, together with the name of his or her class if necessary.

Links with the EYFS
Related themes – People who help us; Colours; Families
PSED: Talk about the importance of keeping together as a group when away from your setting.

CL: Read some *Postman Pat* stories and talk about the job of a postal worker.

A walk to the supermarket

Write a shopping list, walk to the nearest supermarket, buy some goodies and share a snack together. Then open a supermarket in your role-play area!

What you need:

▶ Permission from parents/carers to take children for a walk

▶ Extra adults to accompany children to increase effectiveness of learning opportunities

▶ A shopping list

▶ Equipment for a role-play supermarket

What you do:

▶ Make arrangements with a local supermarket for your visit. Ask for a member of staff to show the children round some features if there is a bakery or café in the store, for instance. It is best to take the children in small groups, so you may need to make several trips!

- ▶ Talk about what the children expect to see, hear, smell, feel and taste.
- ▶ Make a shopping list with the children before the visit. It's a good idea to choose something specific to buy, such as the ingredients for a sandwich, a healthy fruit salad or some delicious soup, so that the visit is more focussed.
- ▶ Try lots of mathematical activities in the supermarket; for example, ask children to help count five carrots into a bag, compare the size of bags of rice and the weight of different melons, look for numbers on signs, count bottles or tins on a shelf, and look for different 3D shapes such as cylinders, cuboids etc.
- ▶ Point out different signs and read labels and packaging. Extend vocabulary, introducing words such as 'carton', 'dairy' and 'aisle', alongside the names of any unusual fruit and vegetables.
- ▶ Encourage the children to share their feelings and observations, such as how cold it is in the freezer aisle, the delicious smell of baking bread, the sound of the intercom and the bright lights.
- ▶ Back in your setting, set up a supermarket in the role-play area and provide lots of empty food boxes, plastic fruit and veg, salt dough cakes and biscuits, signs and labels, a shopping trolley, baskets and bags, cash tills, purses and coins, scales, etc.

Further afield:

- ▶ Arrange for your local council to provide a bottle bank outside your school for a while so that children and parents can get involved in recycling. Talk about the importance of recycling and caring for our environment. What do the children recycle at home (paper, plastic, glass, food waste, etc.)?

Whatever next?
Buy fresh fish such as a rainbow trout at the supermarket and let children use all their senses to explore it back at your setting. Let them feel the scales on the fish, smell the fish, look at the different parts, feel the bones inside and, after cooking, encourage them to taste the fish.

Links with the EYFS
Related themes: People who help us; Shopping; Food; Growth
PSED: Talk about the importance of keeping together as a group when away from your setting. Remind the children what to do if they get separated from their group.

CL: Share some stories about shopping – you may like to try *The Shopping Basket* by John Burningham and *Shopping with Dad* by Matt Harvey.

A walk to the library

Go on a walk to the nearest library to find out how it works. Encourage the children to choose some books to loan out and take back to your setting.

What you need:

▶ Permission from parents/carers to go on a walk
▶ Extra adults to accompany children to increase effectiveness of learning opportunities
▶ A local library with a children's section
▶ Lots of different types of books
▶ Library card
▶ Old or toy computer
▶ Pen and string

What you do:

▶ Arrange the visit with a local library and ask the librarian to speak to the children about using their service. It is best to take the children in small groups so you may need to make several trips!

▶ Ask children how many of them already visit the local library to borrow books. Talk about what the children expect to see, hear, smell and touch during the walk and their time at the library. Talk about how to behave in a library – keeping quiet, no running about, taking care with books, etc.

▶ At the library, let children share books with a partner. Read some stories to a small group. Ask children to find books about different topics.

▶ Show the children how to use the library card to borrow a selection of books and take them back to your setting.

▶ Set up a library in the role-play corner for children to use. Create a comfortable reading corner with cushions for children to sit on as they read. Set up a librarian's desk with a computer screen and a pen on a piece of string for children to pretend to scan the books.

▶ Make a display of the children's favourite storybooks.

Further afield:

▶ Look at images online of some world famous libraries such as the Library of Congress, Washington, Sansovino Library in Venice, George Peabody Library in Baltimore, Central Library Seattle, Rijkmuseum in Amsterdam and Trinity College Library in Dublin.

Whatever next?

Open a real setting library so parents can borrow books about childcare and children can borrow books to take home and read with their families. Alternatively, organise a book stall and ask for families to donate books to sell on, to raise money to buy new books.

Links with the EYFS

Related themes – People who help us; Books; Ourselves; Opposites

PSED: Talk about the importance of keeping together as a group when away from your setting.

CL: Organise regular opportunities for parents to come into your setting and read to the children.

L: Start a 'Reading Champions' project in your setting.

M: Create a pictogram of children's favourite storybooks.

A walk to the allotment

Visit a local allotment and help children to experience digging, weeding, watering, and harvesting!

What you need:

- ► Permission from parents/carers to take children for a walk
- ► Extra adults to accompany children to increase effectiveness of learning opportunities
- ► Clipboards, paper and pencils
- ► Sketch pads
- ► Digital camera
- ► Suitable clothes
- ► Access to a local allotment plot and a friendly gardener!
- ► A small garden plot, potato tubers and tools

What you do:

- ► Find a suitable allotment to visit by asking parents, friends and local contacts.

▶ Explain to the children what allotments are. They are plots of land rented to people to grow vegetables and flowers, and were very popular after the First World War.

▶ Show the children where you are going on an enlarged map or Google Maps on the IWB. Talk about the route that you will take to get there. Will you have to cross a road? What do they expect to see on the way? Throughout the walk, let children take it in turns to take a photo using the digital camera.

▶ Talk to the children about what they expect to see, hear, smell, touch and taste on this walk. Provide each child with a clipboard, paper and a pencil.

▶ At the allotment, invite children to ask questions about the different plants they can see. Can they name some of the vegetables? How does the gardener care for the plants? Which tools does the gardener use?

▶ If possible, arrange for some of the children to have an opportunity to dig, weed, water and pick produce.

▶ Ask them to sketch what they can see. Is there a shed? Is there a water butt? Is there a path?

▶ Back at your setting, invite children to draw a plan of the allotment showing some of the different plants. Display these together with photos taken on the walk.

Further afield:

▶ Make a collection of fruit and vegetables from all over the world for children to feel, name, smell and taste. Ask parents or children from different cultures to share some of their favourite foods with the rest of the group.

Whatever next?

Try growing some potatoes. Start in February by putting potato tubers into egg boxes with the eyes facing upright. Leave on a windowsill for a few weeks until green shoots appear, and then plant in a sack or old bucket half-filled with compost or plant them in deep trenches in the vegetable patch, with the shoots pointing upright. Cover with more soil and protect the young shoots with more compost as they grow. Harvest your potatoes in early summer.

Links with the EYFS

Related themes – Growth; Gardens; Food

PSED: Talk about the importance of keeping together as a group when away from your setting.

EAD: Sing the traditional song 'One potato, two potato'. Change the words to include different fruit and vegetables. Try 'banana', 'tomato', or 'courgette'!

A walk to the building site

Go on a walk to a nearby building site where children can watch people and machines at work. Then open a building site in your role-play or outdoor area!

What you need:

- ▶ Safe access or sight of a building site
- ▶ Hard hats, gloves and hi-vis jackets
- ▶ Digital camera
- ▶ Microphone and recorder/tablet
- ▶ Sketch paper and clipboards
- ▶ Cardboard boxes, newspaper, tape, sugar paper

What you do:

- ▶ Find a local building site where the children can safely observe the work going on and ask questions of the workers. If your setting is undergoing some building work, this is too good an opportunity to miss!

- Provide hard hats and hi-vis jackets for the children to wear. Stand in a safe place and watch the different machines operating. Talk to the children about what they can see. What different jobs can they see going on? What do they think is being built on this site?

- Ask groups of children to choose a particular machine to watch and sketch – diggers, loaders, cement mixers, cranes, etc. Can they ask the driver about his work and record his answers? Try recording the sounds of the different machines.

- Back at your setting, let the groups of children work together to construct models of some of the machines using junk materials. Use the recorded sounds to create sound effects for the models.

- Make some pretend bricks by stuffing different-sized cardboard boxes with newspaper, taping them shut and then wrapping them in different coloured sugar paper.

- Set up a role-play building site using the homemade bricks, plus other building materials such as plastic, wooden and house bricks, piping, sand, buckets, spades, trowels, wheelbarrows, plans and plumb-lines, all set out on large plastic sheets. Let the children dress up in the hard hats, gloves and hi-vis jackets and role-play working on the site.

- What can they build with these materials? How high a wall can they build using the cardboard bricks? Can they turn a drawing or plan into a real building?

Further afield:

- Go to www.bbc.co.uk and look at Primary Geography; play the games about buildings or homes.

Whatever next?

Place small pieces of safe building materials, such as sand, gravel, canvas, wood, brick pieces, tiles, slate and clay, in a tuff spot or sand tray. Let children handle the materials and compare them. Discuss how they could be used to build structures or buildings. Encourage children to try building and constructing with the materials. Can they use water to mix or blend them with their fingers, spoons and small clay tools?

Links with the EYFS

Related themes – Buildings; Houses and homes, People who help us

PSED: Talk about the importance of keeping together as a group when away from your setting.

CL: Share the book *Busy Building Site* by Amanda Archer, and let the children take turns to lift the flaps and see what the different machines are doing.

A walk to the pet shop

Challenge the children to complete a game of 'I spy' at the pet shop, then on your walk back discuss which animals they spotted!

What you need:

- ▶ Permission from parents/carers to take children for a walk
- ▶ Extra adults to accompany children to increase effectiveness of learning opportunities
- ▶ Digital camera
- ▶ Clipboards, check lists and pencils
- ▶ Access to Google Maps

What you do:

- ▶ Contact the pet shop and arrange a date for your visit. It is best to take the children in small groups, so you may need to make several trips!

- Show the children where you are going on an enlarged map or Google Maps on the IWB. Talk about the route that you will take to get there. Will you have to cross a road? How near is the pet shop to your setting?

- Before you leave the setting, talk to the children and adults about what you expect to see, hear, smell and touch at the pet shop. Check whether any children have any allergies to animal fur. Are there any particularly nervous children who may be alarmed by some pets?

- Encourage children to prepare questions for the shopkeeper and to listen carefully to answers. Remind children not to be noisy in the shop or they will scare the animals.

- At the pet shop, ask children to look out for specific things to tick off on their check list such as two hamsters, three mice, one rabbit, fish, cages, hay, cat food, a dog basket, etc.

- Back at your setting, open a pet shop in the role-play corner. Encourage children to act as pet owners, shopkeepers, or animals! Provide small cages, pet food, soft toy animals, baskets, posters and leaflets about caring for pets.

- Make some small 'pets' such as hamsters, gerbils and mice to occupy the pet shop. Stuff grey or brown socks with old tights, tie off the end, sew on buttons for eyes and circles of felt for ears and nose. Build cages using construct-o-straws or similar.

Further afield:

- Find out about more unusual pets such as lizards, snakes, stick insects, goats, tortoises, hedgehogs, pigs etc. Look at pictures and talk about how to look after different types of animals.

Whatever next?

Talk about how many of the children have pets at home. Conduct a survey to find out which is the most common pet, then make a pictogram to show the results. Set up a fish tank or buy a hamster for your setting so all the children can be involved in caring for a pet.

Links with the EYFS

Related themes – Animals; Birds; Habitats; Ourselves

PSED: Talk about the importance of keeping together as a group when away from your setting. Show sensitivity to needs of others including animals.

CL: Share some stories about pets such as *The Great Pet Sale* by Mick Inkpen, *I want a pet* by Lauren Child and *Funnybones: The Pet Shop* by Allan Ahlberg.

A walk to the baker's shop

Visit a local baker's shop and choose some bread to take back to your setting. Try lots of different breads from all around the world.

What you need:

▶ Permission from parents/carers to take children for a walk
▶ Extra adults to accompany children to increase effectiveness of learning opportunities
▶ A local bakery or bakery department in the local supermarket
▶ Ingredients for baking bread and access to a kitchen

What you do:

▶ Contact a local bakery and arrange a date for your visit. It is best to take the children in small groups, so you may need to make several trips!

- ▶ Show the children where you are going on an enlarged map or Google Maps on the IWB. Talk about the route that you will take to get there. Will you have to cross a road? How near is the bakery to your setting?
- ▶ Talk to the children about what they expect to see, hear, smell, touch and taste during this trip.
- ▶ At the bakery, children may observe how breads and cakes are made first-hand. Ask lots of open questions about what they can see and smell. Invite them to ask questions of the staff at the bakery, too.
- ▶ How many different types of bread and cakes can the children see for sale? What is the most expensive item? Let them choose a loaf of bread to buy and take back to your setting.
- ▶ Set up a bakery in the role-play area of your setting. Provide aprons, hats, a cash register, plastic money, paper bags and lots of salt flour dough bread, cakes and biscuits to buy and sell.
- ▶ Together, sing and act out the traditional song 'Five currant buns in the baker's shop'.

Further afield:

- ▶ Make or buy a collection of breads from around the world for the children to sample such as pitta, chapati, naan, baguette, ciabatta, soda bread, tortilla, bagel, grissini, rye bread, etc. Which is the most popular of these different breads with the children?
- ▶ Display a world map and show the children where all these different types of bread originated from.

Whatever next?
Read the traditional story of 'The Little Red Hen'. Try some baking with the children. Make some bread rolls. The children can be involved with weighing and measuring ingredients, mixing and kneading. Share the bread together at snack time.

Links with the EYFS

Related themes – Food; Harvest

CL: Develop speaking and listening skills in the role-play bakery.

PD: Make sure that children are aware of how to keep themselves safe when away from the setting – staying with their grown up, taking care near busy roads, etc.

M: Children can handle money in the real and role-play bakery.

Minibeast walk

Once in the outdoor area, challenge the children to hunt for minibeasts! Allow them to carefully examine them using a magnifying glass, before returning the creatures to their homes. Build a minibeast mansion.

What you need:

▶ A suitable outside area, garden or park, where minibeasts can be observed
▶ Magnifying glasses and pots
▶ Clipboards, paper and pens
▶ Digital camera

What you do:

▶ Find a suitable outside area for children to explore minibeasts, such as the setting garden or grounds, a local park, garden or field.

- Before setting off, talk about where the children should look – on plants, particularly the underside of leaves, under stones, on tree trunks, in the air, inside flowers, etc. Take care to put back any stones or logs that are lifted up.
- Ask the children to record what they see by drawing a picture or taking a photo.
- Talk about the names of different minibeasts. Enjoy learning new words and names together. How many minibeasts can the children identify?
- Help children to look carefully at minibeasts in more detail, using magnifying glasses. Choose a few bugs to carefully place in a magnifying pot to take back to your setting for closer observation. Take care to return the creatures to the environment after observation.
- Try some minibeast paintings, and make some minibeast models using a variety of collage materials such as pipe cleaners, wooden pegs, netting, materials, beads, tissue paper, painting, etc. Alternatively, make bugs from play dough or clay.

Further afield:

- Visit www.ictgames.com/minibeasts.html and let children have fun making minibeasts online.
- Check out the strangest insects in the world, using books and the internet as resources.

Whatever next?

Build a minibeast mansion in a damp, quiet area, away from play areas and noise. Layer wooden pallets on top of each other and invite small groups of children to fill the gaps in between with a mixture of materials such as straw, leaves and twigs, pieces of bricks, clay tiles, pebbles, logs, pinecones, old guttering pipes, small lengths of canes and terracotta flowerpots lying on their sides. After a few weeks you will notice the minibeast mansion will be full of exciting bugs enjoying their new home!

Links with the EYFS

Related themes – Minibeasts; Animals

PSED: Talk about the importance of keeping together as a group when away from your setting. Show sensitivity to the needs of other creatures.

CL: Read lots of stories about minibeasts – try *The Hungry Caterpillar* or *The Bad-Tempered Ladybird* by Eric Carle, or poems in *Mad about Minibeasts* by Giles Andreae.

Section three: Making it real

A visit from the police

Organise a visit from a local police officer to talk to the children about their work, 'Stranger danger' and road safety.

What you need:

▶ A local police officer who is happy to come and visit your setting and talk to the children
▶ Dressing up clothes
▶ Digital camera
▶ Ink pad, lipstick, clear sticky tape
▶ 'Wanted' posters
▶ Sit and ride toys

What you do:

▶ Talk to the children about what they think the police service does for us. Explain that a police officer is coming to visit your setting and make a list of questions to ask.

- Ask the police officer to talk about topics related to keeping safe such as 'stranger danger' and road safety.
- Let the children dress up in police uniforms, hi-vis jackets, boots, helmets, etc.
- Set up a role-play prison and invite the children to role-play police officers and criminals; set challenges, e.g. can they run fast enough to catch the burglar? Can they help an old lady find her purse? Use ride-on toys as police cars.
- Show the children how to take photos of the 'criminals' using the digital camera.
- Let them make 'wanted' posters of people they need to catch by drawing or painting portraits and offering rewards.
- Take some fingerprints using an ink pad or lipstick. Alternatively, you could take a pencil and scribble heavily on a piece of paper; ask the child to firmly press their index finger in the pencil mark and rock it gently from side to side, then ask them to lift their finger. Put a piece of tape over the finger, press down and gently peel off the tape. Look at the different patterns – whorls, loops and arches.
- At the end of the visit, the children may even get the chance to sit in the real police car and turn on the blue light and siren!

Further afield:

- What would the children do if they ever got lost or separated from their grown up when out? Talk about how important it is to look for a grown up they can trust, such as a police officer in uniform.

Whatever next?

Chalk a giant zebra crossing on the ground outside, or use black and white cardboard indoors. Add some roads, trees etc. Let the children drive around on sit and ride toys and take turns to role-play being police officers directing the traffic and helping children to cross the road. Make some giant traffic lights for the children to operate as they direct the traffic. Set up some roadworks with road signs, cones, tapes, etc. to develop the activity further.

Links with the EYFS

Related themes – People who help us; Transport

PSED: Children can play co-operatively in the police role-play scenarios and take turns with others.

CL: Children should remember to listen attentively to the visitors and ask appropriate questions. Read how Mog manages to foil a burglar in *Mog the forgetful Cat* by Judith Kerr!

PD: Talk about ways to keep safe, particularly around traffic.

A visit from the Fire Service

Arrange for a fire engine and firefighters to visit your setting. Let the children dress up in uniform and learn about the job of a firefighter.

What you need:

▶ Digital camera
▶ Paper and painting equipment
▶ Dressing up clothes

What you do:

▶ Arrange for a fire engine and firefighters to visit from your local fire station. Talk to the children before the visit about questions they would like to ask and things they would like to do.

- Let the children try on firefighter hats, and talk about the safety clothes and high visability colours.
- The children may be able to observe the hose being used and talk about the other equipment on the engine. They could also take turns to sit in the engine and switch on the siren. Take extra care of any very nervous children who may be alarmed by loud noises or the idea of a fire in the building.
- Ask the firefighters to talk to children about what they should do if they hear a smoke or fire alarm at nursery school or home. Arrange a fire practice at your setting. All the children need to know where to go and how to behave if there is an emergency.
- Invite one of the firefighters to pose for a photo next to the fire engine, and later encourage the children paint pictures of it.
- Set up an obstacle course in the outside area for the children to use so they train to be super fit firefighters. Can they complete the obstacle course wearing firefighter uniforms and big boots?

Further afield:

- Talk to the children about the importance of keeping safe near fireworks. Bring in some sparklers and show children how to hold them carefully wearing gloves. Remind them not to touch the sparks and to put the dead sparklers into a bucket of cold water. Can they write their name in the sky with the sparklers?

Whatever next?

As well as reminding children to keep away from fire, it's important to tell them what to do if their clothing ever catches fire. Show the children the 'stop, drop and roll' technique – stop moving, drop to the ground, lie down, put hands up to face and roll.

Links with the EYFS

Related themes – People who help us; Colours; Vehicles

PSED: Children can play co-operatively and take turns with others.

CL: Children should remember to listen attentively to the visitors and ask appropriate questions.

PD: Talk about the importance of exercise for keeping healthy.

A visit from the vet

Invite an animal expert or charity to come and talk to the children about caring for different animals.

What you need:

- Information about vets or other people who work with animals
- A visitor who can bring a range of animals to your setting for the children to look at, handle and learn about (try your local vets; alternatively, The Animal Experience are a company that specialise in school visits: www.animalexperience.org
- Digital camera
- A variety of painting and collage materials
- Equipment to set up a vet's surgery

What you do:

- Let parents and carers know about the visit and check if any of the children have allergies or particular fears and anxieties connected to animals.

- Before the visit, talk to the children about the animals they expect to see and prepare any relevant questions for them to ask their visitor.
- During the session, support any nervous children by sitting next to them and constantly reassuring them.
- Ask the visitor to talk about which animals the children would expect to see in their neighbourhood: in a town, these may include domestic cats, dogs and other pets, birds, hedgehogs, squirrels and foxes; in the country, they may see farm animals, mice, rabbits, ducks, frogs, badgers, deer etc.
- Help the children to choose a favourite animal to paint or make a collage of.
- Go for a walk to the local park to feed the ducks. What other animals might you see on your walk or at the park?
- Open a vet's surgery in the role-play area. Provide soft toy animals, baskets, weighing scales, animal food products, chairs, magazines, dressing up outfits etc.

Further afield:

- Make a list of the children's favourite animals. Talk about where the animals live. Look at a world map and pin small photos of different animals onto the relevant countries.
- Talk about animal habitats, introducing key terminology. Play a matching game using images of animals and their homes, e.g. spider/web, bird/nest, squirrel/tree, rabbit/burrow, bee/hive, fish/stream, dog/kennel, for the children to make pairs.
- Go to www.bbc.co.uk/bitesize/ks1/science and play 'Enviro Spotter'.

Whatever next?
Find out about wild animals that might be living in your neighbourhood. Let the children create fact sheets about their favourite, with pictures and interesting information. Talk about nocturnal animals, and discuss whether any of the animals in your local area are endangered.

Links with the EYFS

Related themes – Animals; Habitats; Birds; Minibeasts
PSED: Children should show sensitivity to needs of others, including animals.
CL: Children should remember to listen attentively to visitors and ask appropriate questions. Read *Noisy Neighbours* by Ruth Green. All the different animals have their own type of noise that disturbs the hero of the book, a tired and grumpy snail.

A visit from the dentist

Arrange for a local dentist to come to your setting and talk about caring for teeth. Open a dental surgery in the role-play area.

What you need:

▶ A friendly dentist who is happy to visit your setting and talk to the children about caring for their teeth

▶ Yoghurt pots that have two sections

▶ White shiny paper and glue

What you do:

▶ Organise a visit from a local dentist who is happy to come and talk to the children about dental hygiene. Inform parents of the visit and invite them to come and join you on the day.

- ► Talk to the children about any prior experiences they may have had of going to the dentist's. Make a list of questions that the children would like to ask your visitor.
- ► Talk about brushing teeth and how important it is to clean your teeth regularly – usually after breakfast and before going to bed. Talk about baby teeth, the Tooth Fairy, permanent teeth, gums, different names of teeth, etc. Show children the best way to brush their teeth.
- ► Introduce the dentist and let the children listen and then ask questions.
- ► Set up a pretend dentist's chair, preferably a reclining or swivelling chair, and invite children to take turns to come and sit on it. Let the children dress up in white coats and wear surgical masks over their mouths.
- ► Make a list of food or drinks that have a lot of sugar in which can damage teeth. Talk about a healthy diet and when it's best to eat sweet treats.
- ► Set up a dental surgery in the role-play area with the special chair, dressing up clothes and lots of soft toys and dolls as patients!

Further afield:

- ► Sign up online with the 'Stop the Rot' campaign to show parents that you are committed to helping young children care for their teeth.
- ► Look at the teeth of different animals. Explain about different types of teeth and their uses.

Whatever next?
Make 'moving mouths' using yoghurt pots with two sections that can be made to open and close. Let children stick a selection of white shiny paper teeth onto the top and bottom jaws. Can the children make their puppets speak or say a tongue twister, such as 'red lorry, yellow lorry'?

Links with the EYFS

Related themes – People who help us; Food; Keeping healthy; Growth
PSED: Children can play co-operatively and take turns with others.
CL: Children should remember to listen attentively to the visitors and ask appropriate questions.
EAD: Sing 'All I Want for Christmas is my two front teeth'.

A visit to Africa

Hold an 'African Day' and enjoy finding out about the geography and culture of different African countries.

What you need:

▶ A staff member, parent or friendly adult who can visit your setting and talk about Africa.

▶ Digital camera

▶ Paper, cotton wool buds and paint

▶ Paper plates

What you do:

▶ Let parents and carers know that you are holding an Africa Day. Talk about your special visitor. Invite any families to bring in photos or artefacts from or about Africa.

- ▶ Talk to the children about the visitor and make a list of questions that the children would like to ask.
- ▶ Invite your visitor to talk to the children about Africa, sharing information about geography, clothes, food, music, festivals, special buildings, etc. What do they most like about Africa? What do they not like?
- ▶ Look at images of African patterns, designs and masks. Ask children to make their own repeated patterns using cotton wool buds and brighly coloured paints. Cut eyeholes into paper plates and use these as African masks, which the children can decorate.
- ▶ Try some African food at snack time – check beforehand for any allergies.
- ▶ Find out about some African animals – lions, monkeys, giraffes, zebras, elephants etc. Let children choose their favourite animal to draw, paint and make a fact file on.
- ▶ Listen to some African music by Youssou N'Dour or Salif Keita. Watch some clips on www.youtube.com from *The Lion King*. Sing along with 'Circle of Life'.
- ▶ Use some African drums or djembes with the children. Alternatively, use empty biscuit tins, baby milk tins, and even cardboard boxes with wooden spoons. Can the children use the drums to play rhythms and send messages?

Further afield:
- ▶ Go to www.africa.com and check out Africam – the online interactive African wildlife safari. Look at images of African animals.

Whatever next?
Make some African yam or sweet potato soup. Pass around the raw sweet potatoes for the children to handle. Ask questions, such as 'What do they feel like?' Help children to peel, chop and fry the sweet potatoes. Add some onions and stock and cook until tender. Blend and serve with chapatis.

Links with the EYFS

Related themes – Food; Animals; Ourselves

PSED: Children can show sensitivity to others' needs and feelings, and form positive relationships with adults and other children.

CL: Remind the children to listen attentively to the visitors and ask appropriate questions.

A visit to China

Hold a 'Chinese Day' and learn about Chinese writing, music, and the traditional story behind Chinese New Year.

What you need:

- A staff member, parent or friendly adult who can visit your setting and talk about China.
- Digital camera
- Paper, brushes and ink

What you do:

- Let parents and carers know that you are holding a China Day. Talk about your special visitor. Invite any families to bring in photos or artefacts from or about China.
- Talk to the children about the visitor and make a list of questions that the children would like to ask.

- ▶ Invite your visitor to talk to the children about China, sharing information about geography, clothes, food, music, festivals, special buildings, etc. What do they most like about China?
- ▶ Show the children some Chinese characters and lettering. Let them use paintbrushes and ink to try and copy some Chinese writing. Find out how to say 'hello', 'goodbye' or 'Happy New Year' in Chinese.
- ▶ Tell the children the traditional story of the Chinese New Year, then act it out together. The animals took part in a race to show off to their Emperor, and the first twelve animals to finish the race were each rewarded by having a year of the Chinese Zodiac named after them. You can read the story together here: www.topmarks.co.uk/ChineseNewYear/ZodiacStory.aspx.
- ▶ You can also find out which Year of the Zodiac the children were born in using the link above. Find out what the features were of that year.
- ▶ Celebrate Chinese New Year with the children. Decorate your setting with red paper lanterns, Chinese posters and more.
- ▶ Find out about giant pandas, which are native to China. What do they like to eat? Listen to some bamboo flute music on YouTube, and watch some clips from the film *Kung Fu Panda*.
- ▶ Try playing a traditional Chinese game, 'Dragon's Tail', with the children. It works best with a group of at least 10 children. Ask them to stand in a line with their arms on the shoulders or waist of the child in front. The first child is the dragon's head and must try to catch the last child, who is the dragon's tail.

Further afield:

- ▶ Visit www.topmarks.co.uk/ChineseNewYear/DragonDance.aspx and watch a film of a Chinese Dragon Dance to celebrate Chinese New Year.

Whatever next?
Organise a walk to your local Chinese restaurant or takeaway. Take small groups of children each time. Arrange for the children to be allowed some Chinese food to sample such as fried rice, seaweed and sweet and sour pork or chicken balls.

Links with the EYFS

Related themes – Food; Animals; Celebrations; Ourselves
PSED: Children can show sensitivity to others' needs and feelings, and form positive relationships with adults and other children.

CL: Remind the children to listen attentively to the visitors and ask appropriate questions.

A visit to India

Organise an 'India Day' and learn about the different clothes, henna patterns, food, music and native animals.

What you need:

- ▶ A staff member, parent or friendly adult who can visit your setting and talk about India
- ▶ Digital camera
- ▶ Paper, pens and paint
- ▶ Indian food
- ▶ Clay and tea lights

What you do:

- ▶ Let parents and carers know that you are holding an India Day. Talk about your special visitor. Invite any families to bring in photos or artefacts from or about India.

- ▶ Talk to the children about the visitor and make a list of questions that the children would like to ask.
- ▶ Invite your visitor to talk to the children about India, sharing information about geography, clothes, food, music, festivals (Hindu, Sikh or Islam), special buildings, etc. What do they most like about India? What do they not like?
- ▶ Show the children how to put on a sari and let them have a go. Look at some henna patterns online and talk about different celebrations. Ask them to draw around their hand on a piece of paper and let them design their own patterns using felt pens. Some children could have patterns drawn on their hands using washable paint or pens.
- ▶ Try some Indian food at snack time; share poppadoms, naan breads, samosas and bhajis. Cook some rice with the children. Let them smell some different spices such as cumin and coriander.
- ▶ Find out about tigers, elephants and other Indian animals. Look at some famous paintings of tigers such as 'Tiger in a Tropical Storm' by Henri Rousseau. Let the children paint their own pictures of tigers.
- ▶ Listen to some Indian music such as 'Raga Rasia' by Ravi Shankar. Watch some Indian dancing on YouTube.

Further afield:

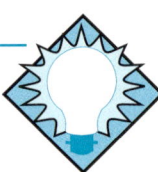

- ▶ Go to www.kids.nationalgraphic.com and look at images of India online such as the Taj Mahal, the Indian flag, elephants, Holi festival, etc.

Whatever next?

Talk about the festival of Diwali. Explain that the children are going to make divas. Provide each child with a ball of clay. Let them handle the clay, squeezing, squashing and rolling it until it is softer to mould. Show them how to shape the clay into a shallow bowl big enough to hold a tea light, pinching the edges around the side. Leave the clay pot to dry and then paint with glitter paint.

Links with the EYFS

Related themes – Food; Animals; Celebrations; Ourselves

PSED: Children can show sensitivity to others' needs and feelings, and form positive relationships with adults and other children.

CL: Remind the children listen attentively to the visitors and ask appropriate questions.

A visit to the UK

Organise a special 'UK Day' and explore the different traditions from England, Wales, Scotland and Northern Ireland.

What you need:

▶ A staff member, parent or friendly adult who can visit your setting and talk about different parts of the UK.

▶ Digital camera

▶ Cardboard, egg boxes, plastic pots, glue and paint

What you do:

▶ Let parents and carers know that you are holding a UK Day. Talk about your special visitor. Invite any families to bring in photos or artefacts from or about England, Wales, Scotland or Northern Ireland.

▶ Talk to the children about your visitor and make a list of questions that the children would like to ask.

▶ Invite your visitor to talk to the children about their part of the UK, sharing information about geography, flags, clothes, food, music, festivals, customs, special buildings, etc. What do they most like about Wales, Scotland or Northern Ireland?

▶ Look at pictures online of national costumes and symbols – Welsh dragons, Scottish kilts, Irish leprechauns, the daffodil, the thistle, the shamrock etc. Learn about the stories behind the patron saints of England, Northern Ireland, Scotland and Wales.

▶ Share some different foods such as Welsh cakes, Scottish porridge or Irish soda bread. Which regional food do the children like best?
Listen to some traditional Scottish or Northern Irish music on YouTube.

Further afield:

▶ Go to www.bbc.co.uk/wales/history/sites/kids/myths and share some Welsh myths with the children.

▶ Go to www.visitscotland.com and find out about famous sights and people of Scotland.

▶ Go to www.irishcultureandcustoms.com and discover interesting facts about Ireland.

Whatever next?
Work together as a group to create a display of a Welsh red dragon. Look at images of dragons in books and online. Draw a huge outline on cardboard of a dragon and attach egg boxes, plastic yoghurt pots and cups to create a spiny, bumpy dragon skin! Let children paint the model with red paint.

Links with the EYFS
Related themes – Food; Celebrations; Ourselves; Dragons
PSED: Children can show sensitivity to others' needs and feelings, and form positive relationships with adults and other children.
CL: Remind the children to listen attentively to the visitors and ask appropriate questions.

Section four: Special places

A local farm

Take a trip to a local farm and learn all about working on a farm and caring for all the different animals!

What you need:

▶ A suitable local farm or children's petting farm
▶ Permission from parents/carers for their child to go on the trip
▶ Extra adults to accompany children to increase effectiveness of learning opportunities
▶ Sketch pads or clip boards and paper
▶ Digital camera

What you do:

▶ Contact a local farm and organise details for your visit including transport. Show the children where you are going on a map.

- Talk to the children before the trip about what they expect to see, hear, smell and touch at the farm.
- If there is a petting area, remind the children to follow instructions such as washing hands after stroking or feeding the animals, not moving too quickly and using quiet voices.
- Available activities will differ at each farm but make sure to plan the trip carefully, booking any specific events in advance. Suggestions include going on a tractor ride, watching duck or pig races, learning about different types of crops, naming farm animals and their young, etc.
- Ask the children to make a list of all the different animals they spot at the farm.
- Ask the farmer to talk to the children about his work and life on a farm.
- Take lots of photos of the children interacting with the farm animals. Play 'I spy', using the names of animals.
- Paint pictures of some of the animals the children saw on the farm. Mount and display the paintings next to photos from the day.
- Sing some farm songs such as 'I went to visit the farm one day', 'Old MacDonald had a farm', 'Baa baa black sheep' and 'Oats and beans'.

Further afield:

- If you need help finding a farm nearby, contact www.farmsforsettings.org.uk for help. Try www.arkfarm.co.uk – they are a mobile farm who bring the farm animals to you!
- Find out about farming in another country at www.farmafrica.org.
- Look at the different crops grown in farms around the world – sweet potatoes in Tanzania, rice in India, tea in China etc.

Whatever next?

Try some drama activities. Read *Farmer Duck* by Martin Waddell to the children and act out the story. Can the children mime all the different jobs poor Duck has to do on the farm? How do the animals plot together to help Duck? Go into role as one of the animals and organise a meeting to discuss options!

Links with the EYFS

Related themes – People who help us; Food; Animals; Ourselves

PSED: Talk about the importance of keeping together as a group when away from your setting. Show sensitivity to the needs and feelings of animals.

PD: Talk about ways to keep healthy and safe around animals.

A place of worship

Visit a local church, mosque or temple and talk to the children about the special purpose of this building.

What you need:

▶ A local church, mosque or temple
▶ Permission from parents/carers to go on the trip
▶ Extra adults to accompany children to increase effectiveness of learning opportunities
▶ Digital camera
▶ Appropriate clothing for all children and adults (some churches and mosques require head coverings)
▶ Shiny paper, clay, PVA glue

What you do:

▶ Plan the route and decide if it is close enough to walk or whether you need to hire a coach. Look at a local map and show the children the location of the building you are visiting.

- ▶ Before you leave the setting, talk to the children about what they expect to see, hear, smell and feel on this trip.
- ▶ Remind them about behaviour expectations, especially remaining as quiet as possible and not running around. Ask the children what they think people do when they are in a place of worship.
- ▶ Arrange to meet the Priest or Imam at the church or mosque, and ask him or her to talk to the children about their special building.
- ▶ Ask if you are allowed to take photos of special features of the building, such as windows or architecture.
- ▶ Invite the children to sit quietly and try to appreciate the special atmosphere in these grand buildings.
- ▶ Back at the setting, ask the children to talk about their what they remember about of the place of worship. Make a floor plan and use some specific language such as aisle, pillar, altar, pulpit, or domed roof, star and crescent moon, minbar.
- ▶ Listen to some church music and invite children to paint pictures of the building.
- ▶ Learn the finger rhyme 'Here is the church and here is the steeple, look inside and here are the people!'

Further afield: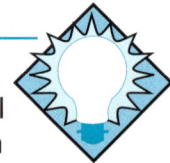

- ▶ Look at pictures of special places of worship around the world such as The Vatican, the Golden Temple in India, St. Basil's Cathedral in Moscow, the Sagrada Familia in Barcelona, The Blue Mosque in Istanbul and York Minster Cathedral.

Whatever next?

Look at some images of mosaics used in special buildings on floors, walls and ceilings. Let the children make their own mosaic patterns using tiny pieces of shiny paper pressed into small square clay titles. Leave to harden and then coat in PVA glue to create a protective varnish. Look at pictures of the stained glass windows. Make your own windows using black sugar paper frames cut into an arch shape and tissue paper glass. Hang in the windows for the sunlight to shine through.

Links with the EYFS

Related themes – People who help us; Ourselves

PSED: Talk about the importance of keeping together as a group when away from your setting.

EAD: Creating mosaic tiles will develop skills using different media and materials.

A special building

Choose a building of architectural or historical significance to visit; then, back in at your setting give children the opportunity to create junk models of the building.

What you need:

▶ A local building of architectural significance or historical interest to visit

▶ Clipboards and sketching equipment

▶ Junk modelling materials

▶ Coloured paper, in a variety of colours

▶ Plain paper, pencils and wax crayons

What you do:

▶ Plan the route and decide if the building is close enough to walk or if you need to hire a coach. Look at a local map and show the children the location of the building you are visiting.

- Before you leave the setting, talk to the children about what they expect to see, hear, smell and feel on this trip.
- Take photos of the children inside and outside the building. Point out special features such as windows, doors, floors, plaques, building materials, etc.
- Talk about its historical significance, if appropriate, e.g. if a famous person lived there or if a historical event took place in the building.
- Invite children to make sketches of the building and take photos of the building from different angles. Let them make rubbings of interesting floor patterns or inscriptions using thin paper and wax crayons.
- Back at your setting, allow children to build models of the building. Can they work together in groups to create a model castle, manor house, tower block or any other building of interest?
- Look at Paul Klee's painting 'The Castle and the Sun'. Let children use coloured paper shapes to create a collage of their favourite special building.

Further afield:

- Look at images of special buildings around the world such as Warwick Castle, the Gherkin in London, the Eiffel Tower in Paris, the Elephant Building in Bangkok, the Egyptian Pyramids, Hundertwasser Haus in Vienna and the Empire State Building in New York. Let the children choose one to paint a picture of for a display.

Whatever next?

Talk about different building materials used in buildings – bricks, wood, glass, metal, wire, tiles, plastic, cement etc. Go to www.brickbuilding.com and use the virtual lego-style bricks to create a magnificent building online. Try some simple wax crayon rubbings of brickwork, pavements, manhole covers and interesting sections of wood.

Links with the EYFS

Related themes – Buildings; Artists; Castles

PSED: Talk about the importance of keeping together as a group when away from your setting.

M: Choose a building to count the different features – windows, floors, doors, towers etc.

EAD: Using a variety of media to produce pictures of special buildings.

The local market

Walk to your local market, talk to the stallholders and support the children in buying fruit and vegetables. Set up your own market in the role-play area.

What you need:

▶ A local market
▶ Phone or tablet to record sounds
▶ Digital camera
▶ Items to set up a role-play market

What you do:

▶ Walk to your local market with small groups of children. Before setting out, talk to the children about what they expect to hear, see, smell, touch and taste.

- ▶ Point out different stalls on the market and what they are selling.
- ▶ Ask the children to listen carefully to the market stallholders as they call out to sell their wares. Record some of the calls to listen back to later.
- ▶ Interview one of the stallholders about their work. How long have they done this job? What do they sell the most of in a week? What don't they like about the job?
- ▶ Buy a selection of vegetables from the stalls. Talk about prices, amounts, types of vegetable, colours, sizes, smells, etc.
- ▶ Back at your setting, work together to make some vegetable soup using the different vegetables you bought at the market. Let the children help by washing, peeling, weighing, chopping and cooking the ingredients. Share the soup at snack-time.
- ▶ Set up a role-play market with different stalls selling fruit, vegetables, jewellery, shoes, bread, toys, etc. Ask the children to dress up and go to the market with their shopping lists, bags, money, etc. Set them challenges, e.g. 'Today you need to buy five oranges, three toy cars and a loaf of bread.'
- ▶ Play a game of 'My Granny went to Market', where you test how many different items the children can recall.

Further afield:

- ▶ Read the story *My Granny went to Market* by Stella Blackstone and Christopher Corr. Travel around the world and practise counting all the different things Granny buys on her travels. Look online at images of the different places she visits.
- ▶ Look at the following painting by L.S. Lowry: 'Market Square, Northern Town'. Invite children to paint their own pictures of the market square that they visited.

Whatever next?

Watch the scene from *Oliver Twist* that features the song 'Who will buy?'. Listen back to some market calls recorded during the market visit. Can the children copy the calls? Can they tell what the trader is shouting? Encourage them to try making up their own calls to use at the role-play market.

Links with the EYFS

Related themes – Shopping; Food; Travel

PSED: Talk about the importance of keeping together as a group when away from your setting.

M: Use everyday language and experiences to handle money when buying items at the real and the role-play market.

The seaside

Organise a trip to your nearest seaside or beach. Look at features of the landscape and local area. Build sandcastles and go beach-combing.

What you need:

▶ A suitable seaside location within easy reach of your setting
▶ Buckets and spades
▶ Digital camera
▶ Appropriate clothing and sun protection

What you do:

▶ Organise the trip with parents and carers, and book transport if necessary. Before the trip, show the children where you are going on a map.

- Talk to the children about what they expect to see, hear, smell and touch at the beach.
- Remind the children to stay with you at all times, and talk about keeping safe near the water.
- Point out features of the landscape: the sea, waves, the horizon, sand dunes, cliffs, rock pools, tidal marks, sea walls, etc. Look at different shells, plants, creatures, pebbles and pieces of driftwood.
- Let children take off their shoes and socks and paddle in the shallows, making sure they are supervised at all times.
- Work in groups to build sandcastles and other sand sculptures. Photograph the results before the sea comes and washes them away!
- Talk about 'beach-combing'. As a group, try creating a giant artwork by drawing an outline using a stick and filling it in with shells, stones, sand and seaweed.
- Enjoy ice creams or a picnic on the beach for snack.
- Take lots of photos so that the children can use them back at your setting to remember their special visit.

Further afield:

- Look at images online of beaches around the world, from Zlatni Rat in Croatia to Trunk Bay in the Virgin Islands National Park.
- Look at images of different seaside creatures. Which ones did they spot on their trip to the beach (crabs, seagulls, sea anemones, starfish, fish, shellfish, etc.)? Encourage them to try painting pictures of some of their favourite coastal or sea creatures.

Whatever next?
Use some of the photos and pictures drawn by the children to create a poster all about your day at the beach. Can the children draw or paint a postcard of their trip to the beach? Encourage them to write a message on the back and send it to a family member or friend.

Links with the EYFS

Related themes – Holidays; Animals
PSED: Talk about the importance of keeping together as a group when away from your setting.
CL: Read *At the Beach* by Roland Harvey, *The Sand Horse* by Ann Turnball and/or some *Seaside Poems* by Jill Bennett.

Now and then

As a group, look at photos of your local area in the past. Organise a 'Grandparents' Day' and invite grandmas and grandads to come and share activities with the children.

What you need:

▶ Pictures of your local neighbourhood, now and in the past
▶ Books about the past
▶ Artefacts such as old toys and books

What you do:

▶ Invite parents, carers and colleagues to bring in photos of the local area from different times in the past.
▶ Go to www.whatwasthere.com and research some images from the past to show the children.

► Talk to the children about what they think the environment was like in the past. Think about transport (cars vs. horses), clothes (trousers vs. breeches) and food (takeaway vs. bread and dripping).

► Organise a grandparents' day at your setting and invite parents and grandparents' to visit and share some activities with the children.

► Do some baking with the children to share with their families. Scones and jam are a great favourite with all ages!

► Invite grandparents to bring in something from their childhood to show the children, such as a book, a game, a photograph or even just a memory. Encourage them to talk to the children about how things have changed.

► Ask grandparents to play some traditional games with the children such as hopscotch, marbles or jacks.

► Learn the rhyme 'Here are Grandma's glasses' and act it out for the grandparents.

Further afield:

► Find out about an important event in the history of your neighbourhood such as a fire, a battle or an associated famous person. Share the details with the children to help them develop an understanding of the past that they can identify with.

Whatever next?
Set up a portrait booth in your setting. Invite grandparents to come and pose for a photograph with their grandchildren. Let children paint portraits of their grandparents. Frame the pictures with 'old-fashioned frames' made from dry pasta stuck on stiff cardboard and sprayed with gold paint.

Links with the EYFS

Related themes – Houses; Transport; Clothes; Food; Toys

PSED: Hosting Grandparents' Day will help children to form positive relationships with adults.

CL: Children listen to stories and visitors and respond with relevant questions.